Faith, Hope and Love

Faith, Hope and Love

Poems of Christian Inspiration by Connie J. Stout

Connie J Stout

City of God Church

CONTENTS

1	Come To The Lord	1
2	Our Dad	3
3	God Walks With Me	5
4	There Is No One Like You Lord	7
5	Hang On	9
6	God's Mercy	11
7	Thank You Lord	13
8	Ask And Believe	15
9	I Am Fine	17
10	Just Call on Jesus	19
11		21
12	A New Year From Jesus	23
13	One Way To Heaven	25

CONTENTS

14 | When the River Runs Empty 27
15 | Thank You Jesus 29
16 | Stars 31
17 | Trust In Jesus 33
18 | Happy Valentine's Day 35
19 | He Is Risen 37
20 | The Lord Has Been So Good To Me 39
21 | Jesus Is With Me 41
22 | There's No One Like You Lord 43
23 | Go Bring My Children Home 45
24 | Give God's Love 47
25 | Why Me Lord? 49
26 | When He Call Me Home 51
27 | Even If I Wanted To 53
28 | It's Going To Be Alright 55
29 | I'll Stick With You 57
30 | Someday 59

CONTENTS

31	Setting At The Feet Of Jesus	61
32	Pay No Attention To What Men Say	63
33	There's A Good Man In My Life	65
34	The Other Side Of Love	67
35	I Need You And I Love You	69
36	Satan Has To Run	71
37	Happy Birthday Son	73
38	What Would I Do?	75
39	My Friend	77
40	I Love You Lord	79
41	Letters To A Soldier	81
42	I'll Never Walk Alone	83
43	He's My Lord And King	85
44	Trust In The Lord	87
45	Covered By The Blood	89
46	Traveler's Lament	91
47	Happy Birthday Mother	93

CONTENTS

48 | No Segregation In Heaven 95

49 | Keys To The Kingdom 97

50 | Jesus Is Lord 99

51 | Who? 101

52 | Jesus Can 103

53 | There's A Difference In Me 105

54 | Lord I Believe 107

55 | Be Of Good Cheer 109

56 | Jesus Loves Me 111

57 | Bright Shines The Sun 113

58 | Someday 115

59 | We'll Be Happy Over There 117

60 | God Takes Care Of His Children 119

61 | In That Bright City 121

62 | I'll Follow Jesus 123

63 | March On Pilgrim 125

64 | He Will Hold Me In His Hand 127

CONTENTS

65 | Speak Not In Anger **129**

66 | God Says To Forgive **131**

67 | Through The Power Of The Blood **133**

68 | Drawing Nigh **135**

69 | I'm Glad I Have A Savior **137**

70 | Colorado **139**

71 | Look At The Fishes **141**

72 | Here Kitty **143**

73 | Love Is **145**

74 | Jesus Takes Care Of Me **147**

75 | Jesus Signed My Pardon **149**

76 | I'm A Winner **151**

77 | Send Down You Love Lord **153**

78 | When We Meet God's Son **155**

79 | The Lord Is Watching Over Me **157**

80 | I'm Going Home Someday **159**

81 | In The Still Of The Night **161**

CONTENTS

82	Let Me Be Ever Ready	163
83	I Love You Lord	165
84	Heaven The Beautiful Land	167
85	I've Been Forgiven	169
86	I'll Never Give Up	171
87	Hold To My Hand	173
88	I Speak Peace To You	175
89	God's Comforting Ways	177
90	I'll Make It Through	179
91	Praise Him	181
92	I'll Take Jesus	183
93	Praise The Name Of Jesus	185
94	Darkness Has To Go	187
95	God's Only Son	189
96	The Choice	191
97	Jesus Can	193
98	Jesus Has Promised A Mansion To Me	195

CONTENTS

99 | The Lord Made The World **197**

100 | All Is Well **199**

101 | **201**

102 | When He calls Me Home **203**

103 | Faith Hope and Love **205**

Copyright © 2020 by Connie J Stout

All rights reserved. No part of this book may be reproduced in any manner whatsoever without written permission except in the case of brief quotations embodied in critical articles and reviews.

First Printing, 2020

1

Come To The Lord

Come one and all to the house of the Lord.
Come everyone and listen to His word.
He died to save us from our sins
So, open your heart and ask Him to come in.
He suffered and died one day at Calvary,
He suffered and died to save you and me.
But on the third day he arose and walked out
of the grave.
He died and arose from the dead, so we all could be saved.
So remember everyone that He loves you.
And He'll do everything that He's promised to do.
He'll stay beside you and give you the victory
Over sin and the grave and give you life eternally.
He'll stay beside you, lead you and guide you
Brother and Sister, and save your loved ones to.
So, pray and ask Him to save them from their sins,
then ask them to pray and open up their hearts
and let Him come in.
Because he loves us one and all

2

Our Dad

He raised his children as best he could
And tried to do what was right and good
He made mistakes as humans do
But never failed to say, I love you
He taught us about the love of God
And lived his faith as here he tried
He gave of himself to his family and friends
Ever faithful to God to the very end
Although we will miss him he is happy I know
In a land free from heartache sorrow and woe
Someday we will meet him in heaven on High
Reunited forever as the endless ages roll by

3

God Walks With Me

God walks with me daily to show me the way
He says follow me and do what I say
And I will bring you through and show you what to do
For you are my child and I love you
He will never forsake me, this one thing I know
So I'm walking with Jesus wherever I go
You too can walk with Him if you open your heart
For he will walk with you and never depart

There Is No One Like You Lord

There is no one like You Lord, No one like You
Help me to remember there is no one like You
When I'm discouraged and I lose my way
Then out of the darkness I hear you say
There's no one like you child
There's no one like you
I have no forgotten
And I'll bring you through
There's no one like You Lord
There's no one like You
Help me to tell others
There's no one like You

5

Hang On

Hang on, God is on the Throne
Hang on, you are not alone,
Hang on, Christians, Hang on.
When your life has crumbled down around your feet,
There's sorrow in your heart,
And all you feel is defeat
God wants you to know
That he's still King of Kings
And He will bring you out
And cause your heart to sing.
So, hang on God is on the Throne,
Hang on, you are not alone,
Hang on Christians, Hang on.

God's Mercy

Without your mercy, Lord where would I be?
Wondering down a dark lonely road.
Bent so low beneath the heavy load.
Without your mercy, where would I be.
The mercy of God has set me free
From heartache, sorrow and strife.
The mercy of God is all I need
To guide me down the dark rocky road of life.
We're gathered to praise His sweet name
When we leave here we'll not be the same.
Jesus hears us and knows us and knows where we are.
If we trust Him He'll fill us with His power.
Many are the afflictions of the righteous
But, the Lord delivers him from them all.
God's mercy delivers us.

Thank You Lord

Thank you Lord for helping me through
This troubled life.
Thank you for leading me from darkness to light.
Thank you for helping me to overcome
The problems of life through faith in Jesus your son.
You give me strength when I start to fall
And lift me up, when your name I call.
There is none like you Lord, no one like you.
Thank you for bringing me through.
Thank you Lord, Thank you Lord, Thank you
Lord, for bringing me through.

Ask And Believe

Whatever you ask in my name you'll receive
All you need to do is ask and believe
Just ask for what you need and for you I'll provide
Just believe in my word and walk by my side
Just walk by my side child and I will give
Whatever you need to help you live
In this world down here where there's so
Much need.
You are my child, so ask and believe.
Ask and believe, ask and believe
You are my child, so ask and believe
And I will provide

9

I Am Fine

The Lord healed me, I am fine, I am fine
And I thank Him for His great love divine
The Lord healed me, He's always there
My Lord healed me because He cares
The Lord protects and provides for me, I am fine,
I am fine
And I thank Him for His blessings divine
The Lord protects and provides for me, He's always there
My Lord protects and provides for me because He cares
The Lord delivered me from sin and shame
The Lord delivered me, Oh! Praise His dear name
The Lord delivered me, He's always there
My Lord delivered me because He cares
The Lord really does care
And He answers our prayers

10

Just Call on Jesus

When dark clouds hover over you
And you don't know what to do
Just call on the name of Jesus
And He will lead you through
He'll shed His light upon you
And turn the darkness into day
Jesus will stay beside you
And He'll guide you all the way
No matter what Satan throws at you
Just bow you head and pray
The Lord will give you victory
And a brighter, brighter day

11

A New Year From Jesus

This is a new year from Jesus
My children don't you fear
Everything will be Ok
I will turn your night into day
Just call upon my name in prayer
And I will take away all your care
Just pray and believe
And my help you'll receive
There's nothing that I can't do
My child, I will take care of you
I died so you could be free
And someday you will be here with me

One Way To Heaven

There's only one way to Heaven
]one way to Heaven and no more
There's only one way to Heaven
Through Jesus Christ our Lord
Yes, there's only one way to Heaven
God said one way to Heaven and no more
If you want to go to Heaven
Open wide, He's knocking at your hearts door
There's only one way to Heaven
One way to reach the golden shore
Oh! There's only one way to Heaven
But, there's always room for more
There's only one way to Heaven
Our Savior has walked this way before
Oh, there's only one way to Heaven
Just follow the footsteps of our Lord

14

When the River Runs Empty

When the river runs empty
Life fades away
When the water stops flowing
There's no joy in the day
Once the river was flowing
And running so strong
Gentle breezes were blowing
And our hearts filled with song
Then the dry season came
And soon the water was gone
Nothing was the same
And gone was the song
So dark was the night
And gone was the sun
It seems we'd lost sight
Of what God had begun
Then down on our knees
To God in Heaven we prayed
We said father please
The draught must be stayed
The flood gates of Heaven He opened
Showers of blessing they fell
Now once again the river runs freely
God brought us through the dry spell

Thank You Jesus

Thank you Jesus for dying for me
Thank you Jesus for setting me free
From the bondage of sin and shame
Oh! Praise Your sweet name
Thank you Jesus for dying for me
You suffered and died on Calvary
Then, on the third day you arose from the grave
So all the world from sin could be saved
Thank You Jesus

16

Stars

Stars in the sky shone down on the earth
As the angels told the shepherds about Jesus birth
A star led the way for the wise men three
To the place where the young child son on
His mother's knees
Yes, the stars were shining so bright
They lit up the dark sky in the middle of
The night
The shepherds were afraid and fell on their knees
An angel said, fear not, we bring good news to thee
In a manger in Bethlehem in a lowly cattle stall
The Son of God was born to fulfill the law
His name is Jesus, Prince of Peace and Emanuel
The father sent him to us to share his love
And to save our souls from Hell

Trust In Jesus

Someday our Lord will call us home
Never more in darkness to roam
We'll spend eternity in Heaven so fair
With God, Jesus and our loved ones waiting there
Sometimes our life seems painful and sad
But, if we call on Jesus, He'll make us glad
He'll always take away the sadness and pain
And help His people to be happy again
So, call on Jesus when life's problems get you down
He'll give you a mansion a robe and a crown
So, serve and trust him while you're here below
And some glad day to Heaven you'll go
Many are the afflictions of the
Righteous but the Lord delivers
Him out of them all

18

Happy Valentine's Day

The first valentine was from God to the world
John 3:16 "For God so loved the world that He gave His only begotten Son that who so ever believeth in Him, should not perish but have everlasting life."
Second valentine was from Jesus to the world.
John 15:13 "Greater love hath no man than this, that He lay down His life for His friends."
This valentine is from me to you
John 13:34, Jesus said "Love one another as I have loved you"
So brothers and sisters I love you
I love you with the love of the Lord
I love you as it says in God's word
Jesus said to "love one another as I have loved you."
So, brothers and sisters I love you
I love you with the love of the Lord
God Bless You
Happy Valentine's Day

He Is Risen

He is risen, He is alive
And seated up above
With the Heavenly Father
And they both send you their love
He died that day on Calvary
So we could be set free
From the chains of sin
So, open up your heart and ask Him to come in
He will stay beside you
And never leave your side
Yes, He will stay beside you
And always be your guide
Through this dark and weary land
And the trials that come your way
Just look up to Him and take hold of His hand
Just trust in Jesus and He will guide you
Through each day
And remember what He said
"I'll never leave you nor forsake you"

The Lord Has Been So Good To Me

The Lord has been so good to me
He takes care of me and my family
He's always there by our side
And someday in Heaven with Him we'll abide
Yes, we'll spend eternity with Christ our Lord
If we believe and obey His word
So, don't let Satan get you down
And someday you'll receive a robe and a crown
The lord is waiting in Heaven for you
And all of life's troubles He'll bring you through
He'll bring us to Heaven one and all
So, keep listening for His call
Someday He'll call us to come home
Never more in darkness to roam
For in Heaven, Jesus is the light
So never more will there be a dark night

Jesus Is With Me

Jesus is walking with me
He helps lead me over life's troubled sea
I'll make it to Heaven if I follow His lead
For Jesus my savior is walking with me
H walks with me daily to show me the way
He says "Follow me and do what I say,"
And I'll bring you through to Heaven
I love you my child and I'll show you the way
My Heavenly Father is there when I call
He picks me up each time that I fall
He gives me the strength to start over again
He is my savior and I love Him
He'll never forsake me this one thing I know
So, I'm walking with Jesus
You too can walk with Him if you open your heart
He will walk with you and never depart

There's No One Like You Lord

There's no one like you Lord, no one like you
Help me to remember there's no one like you
When I'm discouraged and I lose my way
Then out of the darkness I hear you say
There's no one like you child
There's no one like you
I have not forgotten
And I'll bring you through
There's no one like you Lord
There's no one like you
Help me to tell others
There's no one like you

Go Bring My Children Home

On the third day Jesus arose from the grave
He suffered and died, a sinful world to save
Now He's seated with God the Father
On the Heavenly Throne
Just waiting for God to say "Son go bring my
Children home."
Go bring my children home, go bring my
Children home
He's waiting for God to say "Son go bring my
Children home"
If you don't want to be left when He makes
That Heavenly call
Open your Bible and on the Lord do call
Ask Him to forgive all sins
Then when He takes God's children home
Yes, you too can enter in

24

Give God's Love

Take God's love and give it away
To the lost and the lonely
And to those who are hurting today
You may not know what God can do
With these three words – Jesus loves you
There's so many who don't know the Lord
And are needing someone to share the word
So take God's love to your fellow man
And tell them all of Salvations plan
Take God's love and give it away
To everyone you meet today
You never know the pain they feel
So, tell them God loves them and His love is real
Take God's love and give it away
As you travel down life's pathway
You know the joy it will bring
One touch of His love can make a heart sing
Take God's love and give it away
It was put in your heart to stay
To keep some for yourself and share the rest
By giving to others some souls may be blessed

Why Me Lord?

I used to set around all day
And to the Lord I'd pray
And every time I did this
These are the words I'd say
Why me Lord? Why me Lord? Why does this happen
To Me?
Why me Lord? Why me Lord? Why me Lord?
If you loved me you'd protect me Lord
Why should this happen to me?
Then one day while praying this way
The Lord said to me
"I stood before Pilot's court and took the
Abuse that day
I suffered and bled and gung upon a tree
I took the beating and the pain
So someday you'd be free
And not once did I say, Why me Lord?
Why me Lord? Why me Lord? Why?
Does this happen to me?
Why me Lord? Why me Lord? Why should
This happen to me?
Now I understand why sometimes things must be
Just because I go through trials
Doesn't mean God doesn't care for me

CONNIE J STOUT

I love you Lord because I know than you love me
Thank You Lord

When He Call Me Home

My Jesus died so I might live
And all my heart to Him I give
Never more in sin I'll roam
I'll serve Him till He calls me home
When He calls me home, when He calls me home
How I'll rejoice when He calls me home
When He calls me home, when He calls me home
What joy's we'll share when He calls me home
When I feel my burdens get me down
I think of Jesus and the thorn made crown
He wore for me on His head
And His precious blood for me He shed
He let them nail Him to the cross
So my soul would not be lost
Is it any wonder that I say
I'll serve Him till the Judgment Day?
Then I can hardly wait till He
Calls me home

Even If I Wanted To

My heart still thrills each time we kiss
The way it used to do
I could never love anyone like this
Even if I wanted too
The way I feel when you hold me close
And whisper "I love You"
I could never feel this way again
Even if I wanted to
I started out when I was young
Down this road of life with you
I could never walk with someone else
Even if I wanted to
Many years have come and gone
Now we're both turning gray
But I still love you just as much
As I did yesterday
So put your arms around me dear
And hold me close to you
For loving you my whole life through
Is all I want to do

It's Going To Be Alright

It's going to be alright
With Jesus in your heart
He will bring you through
Whatever life imparts
I know it's going to be alright
If you will follow Him
He will cleanse your heart
And make it free from sin
Whenever things look dark
And you don't know what to do
Just look up to Jesus
He's always there with you
It's going to be alright
It's going to be alright
It's going to be alright child
It's going to be alright

I'll Stick With You

I'll stick with you through sickness and in health
Through poverty and wealth
I'll stick with you through the years
That come along
And I'll never do you wrong dear, I'll
Never do you wrong
In my heart there's a song
Because I'll never do you wrong
Forever more I'll bless the day you
Came along
Now my heart is filled with song
A lonely life no more I'll see
Because you're hear with me

30

Someday

I'm going home to Heaven someday
This life is just a stop along the way
Though I walk through many valleys
I know Jesus and a mansion are waiting
In my Heavenly home
Although I sometimes suffer
As I travel on my way
I know my Jesus hears me
And answers when I pray
He walks along beside me
And keeps me safe from harm
And in any time of trouble
He keeps me in the shelter of His arms

Setting At The Feet Of Jesus

I'll be setting at the feet of Jesus
Discussing all the trials of the past
I'll be setting at the feet of Jesus
When I reach my Heavenly home at last
When I reach my heavenly father at last
When I reach my heavenly home at last
I'll be setting at the feet of Jesus
When I reach my heavenly home at last
I'll be shouting down the streets of gold
With my loved ones who've gone on before
I'll be shouting down the streets of glory
Praising God forever and ever more

Pay No Attention To What Men Say

Pay no attention to what men say
Live for me, read your Bible and Pray
It's true what you read in my Hold Book
Man on the outward appearance will look
But God the Father looks at the heart
For that's where all the true feelings are

There's A Good Man In My Life

There's a good man in my life
And he wants me for his wife
There's a good man in my life
And he loves me
All the heartaches and tears
And the loneliness of years
Are forgotten when he holds me in his arms
There's a good man in my life and he loves me

The Other Side Of Love

Bring me your sorrow and your tears
Your sadness and your fears
And the loneliness that you weren't
Meant to bear
I'll give you job for your tears
That will last down through the years
And the happiness that we were meant to share
On the other side of love
I'll give you joy and tenderness
And all the love you've missed
I'll show you how that love was means to be
On the other side of love
On the other side of love
There is joy and happiness beyond compare
So, stay with me and I will take you there
To the other side of love

I Need You And I Love You

Sometimes you don't think I love you
But, God knows that I do
And you don't believe I need you
But darling, that's not true
I need you like a budding rose
Needs the sun and rain
To bring forth it's beauty again and again
I love you like a mother loves her babe
In arms
And I love to lay beside you where I
Feel safe from harm

Satan Has To Run

Satan delights in causing trouble
Trouble to all of God's children
Satan delights in causing trouble
But, when you call on Jesus, Satan has to run
Satan has to run, oh Satan has to run
When "in the name of Jesus" we pray
Satan has to run, oh Satan has to run
For Satan is no match for our God or His Son
Satan has to run, Praise God he has to run
When confronted with God's word
Satan has to run, Praise God he has to run
Yes, he has to run for he is no match
For Our Lord

Happy Birthday Son

Happy birthday to you, my wonderful son
I'm so proud of you and all you have done
You make life much better for others and me
You are the best son that ever could be
So happy birthday to you
And may you have many more
And may each one be better
Than the one before
I love you Mom

What Would I Do?

What would I do if you should leave me?
I'd be lost as a bird without a tree
I'd be blue as the sky without a cloud dear
What would I do if you weren't here?
What would I do if you weren't here today?
What would I do if you weren't here?
I'd be like a world that has no sun
I'd be like the Arctic cold and frozen
What would I do without your love?
I'd be like a night with no stars up above,
Like a sky with no moon to shine the way
I'd be lost if you took your love away
I'd be like the desert with no sand,
I'd be like a clock that has no hands,
I'd be like a poem without a rhyme
For I will love you until the end of time
What would I do without you?

My Friend

The Lord knew that I would need a friend
So He searched the world from end to end
Then he gave us a home just a few blocks apart
And on day our kids introduced us and
That was the start of a special friendship that's
Lasted for years
Through joy and laughter, sorrow and tears
I'm glad you're my friend and just want to say
I hope you have a very, very happy birthday
On this day I want to thank you for being my friend
I pray the very best blessings to you God will send
May He give you good health and happiness too
May you never be lonely, and never be blue
This is my prayer for you my dear friend
Life everlasting and joy without end
May God Bless you always, in all ways

40

I Love You Lord

I love you Lord more than silver and gold
I love you Lord more than riches untold
I love you Lord and I'll always be,
Willing to be used by Thee

41

Letters To A Soldier

Dear Soldier,
Although I've never met you and don't even know
Your name
I'd like to write a letter and thank you
Just the met
I know you have a family, of loved ones, ok,
So dear
And while you're out there fighting they wait
And worry here
I know you had to leave them when you
Country called
Ant that you're out there fighting for freedom
For us all
I would like to thank you and all soldiers brave
And true
For there would be no freedom if not for men and
Women like you
Again I want to thank you, because your
Presence over there
Helps to keep our homeland free, God Bless and
Keep you is my prayer
Sincerely, a thankful to be free
And proud to be American

I'll Never Walk Alone

Sometimes when I'm alone, I just want to cry
And many times I don't even know why
I just feel so sad, so lonely and blue
My life is a mess and I don't know what to do
Sometimes I feel so lost, as if I'd lost my way
And I find it hard to cope with life's troubles everyday
And just when I feel that all hope is gone
Jesus reminds me, I'll never walk alone
I'll never walk alone for He is with me
To help me through my trials with victory
I'll never walk alone, Jesus holds my hand
And someday I'll be walking through in Heaven's fair land

He's My Lord And King

Caring not what comes my way
I'll serve Him till the judgement day
Knowing He will keep me strong
I'll trust Him through the whole day long
For He's My Lord and King
Through the trials I love Him still
Let Satan try just what he will
My Jesus knows just what to do
And He always brings me through
For He's My Lord and King
He saved my soul from hell
Of His mercy I will tell
His love I'll spread abroad
Telling all to come to God
For He's My Lord And King

Trust In The Lord

Trust in the Lord with all of your heart
And from you He will never depart
He'll be with you through the night and the day
And He'll always show you the way

Covered By The Blood

I'm covered by the blood of the Lamb
And protected by the Great I Am
And this one thing I know
That wherever I may go
I'm covered by the blood of the Lamb
Just pray and trust in His word
He'll make everything ok, for God
Is Our Lord

Traveler's Lament

Orange barrels along the highway
Orange barrels to back my way
Every time I take a vacation
It's orange barrels along the way
Big ol' signs say "merging traffic
This lane ends move over please"
Big orange barrels along the highway
In endless rows that never cease
Detour sign says "you can't go here
Turn around and go back there"
So I do just what it tells me
Lord, oh, Lord where am I now?

Happy Birthday Mother

Happy birthday my mother so dear
I thank God in Heaven that you're still here
I thank Him for giving me to you
I love you dear mother, happy birthday to you
I love you Mother

No Segregation In Heaven

There'll be no segregation in Heaven
There'll be no segregation up there
Where everyone you meet is sister or brother
We'll all shout and sing without a care
There'll be no segregation in Heaven
Of the red, yellow, black, brown and white
Jesus died to save everybody
And we are all the same in His sight
There'll be no segregation in Heaven
No segregation on the streets of Gold

Keys To The Kingdom

Keys to the Kingdom
The Lord has given us keys to the Kingdom
Keys to the Kingdom
If in Him we trust
So trust in the Lord
And serve Him night and day
And the keys to the kingdom
Will open Heavens door for you someday?
There you will meet the Lord
Who graciously brought you through,
Believe that you believed His word
And did what He told you too
The keys to the Kingdom
Will open new doors for you
The keys to the Kingdom
Will help bring you through

50

Jesus Is Lord

Jesus is Lord over all, Jesus is Lord over all
He buried my sins deeper than the sea
Jesus is Lord over all
Jesus is Lord over all – Jesus is Lord over all
He's coming back to take us home with Him
Yes, Jesus is Lord over all
I know Jesus is Lord over all, He's proved
He's Lord over all
He heals our disease, forgives all iniquities
Yes, Jesus is Lord over all
I know Jesus is Lord over all, yes He's Lord over all
When He comes back the scoffers will know
Jesus is Lord over all
Yes, when He comes back, to late they will way
That Jesus was Lord after all, and over all

51

Who?

Who loves me anyway
Though, I may falter on my way?
Who loves me anyway?
Nobody but Jesus my Lord
Who stays right by my side
And help me over life's rolling tide?
Who stays right by my side?
Nobody but my Lord
Who takes time to lift me up,
When I've drank from life's bitter cup?
Who takes time to lift me up?
Nobody but Jesus my Lord
And there's one thing I know
When it comes my time to go
Who'll be there to lead me o'er?
Nobody but Jesus my Lord

Jesus Can

Jesus can save you no matter what you've done
Just believe Him and call out in His name
Jesus can heal you no matter what you have
And your life will never be the same
There'll be trials and temptations and burdens
You must bear
If you have faith He will help you through them all
He will walk beside you and hold onto your hand
And He will never let you fall
When earthly friends forsake you and refuse to
Shake your hand
Jesus will always be right there
Jesus still loves you, no matter what you've done
Jesus is a friend who'll always care

53

There's A Difference In Me

There's a difference in me, a difference in me
I've been touched by the hand of the Lord
There's a difference in me, a difference in me
And I now understand His holy word
If I knew that I would die tomorrow
In my heart there would be no sorrow
Yes I would be with Christ my King
And through eternal ages His praises sing

Lord I Believe

Jesus look into my heart and mind
And you will know that I believe,
That you died to save all man kind
And I believe that you died for me
You died for me, so I might be saved
So that I could rise up from the grave
And be with You through eternity
Yes, Lord, I believe that you died for me
I believe that You died for all man kind
So redemption each soul could find
You died to set this whole world free
And Lord, I believe you died for me.
Yes, Lord I believe that you died for me

Be Of Good Cheer

Sometimes the sun goes behind the cloud
And makes the day seem dark and drear
But I fall on my knees and cry out Lord
Oh! Help me Jesus, then He is here
Oh! Lord I'm glad that you appear
Anytime that I call on your name
You put your arms around me, saying "Be of good cheer"
For I will supply your needs through
Sunlight or rain

Jesus Loves Me

My Jesus loves me just as I am
As long as I obey His command
He doesn't care how I look
As big as I live by the words of His book
Jesus has promised a mansion to me
Where I will live through eternity
No pain, so suffering, no tears to be shed
For Jesus paid the price when His precious
Blood was shed

Bright Shines The Sun

Bright shines the sun in my Heavenly home
It shines on the angels and God's great Throne
It shines on my loved ones and the prophets
Who've gone on before
I can hardly wait to reach that bright shore
I can hardly wait till that sun shines on me
I can hardly wait my Jesus to see
He'll be standing there with outstretched hand
To welcome me to that bright shining land

58

Someday

Someday I'm going to see my Savior
Someday I'm going to see my Lord
I believe that I will go to meet Him some glad morning
Because He tells me so in His word
Yes, I believe it when He tells me that He loves me
And I believe it when He says He'll come again
For I know that He has a mansion up in Heaven
That will not be occupied till I arrive
He has a mansion waiting there with my name
Above the door
Where I'll never cry or be hurt anymore
All is peace and joy and love, waiting there for me
Sometimes I can hardly wait to go
When He calls I will gladly say good-bye
To these burdens I have carried for so long
I will leave them at His feet, never more to shed a tear
Then I'll move into my bright eternal home

59

We'll Be Happy Over There

We'll be happy at that meeting over there,
We'll be happy at that meeting over there
We'll be happy at that meeting
Our Lord, friends and loved ones we'll be greeting
We'll be happy at that meeting over there
There will be no sorrow over there,
There will be no sorrow over there
There will be no sorrows
Only glad tomorrows
Will you be at that meeting over there?
Will you be at that meeting over there?
Will you be at that meeting
Will you be one I'm greeting?
Will you be at that meeting over there?
Angels will greet us over there,
Angels will greet us over there
Angels will greet us,
But Christ the Lord will meet us
Angels will greet us over there

God Takes Care Of His Children

God takes care of His children
Takes care of His children everywhere
God takes care of His children
In you time of need, just call on Him in prayer
Call to Him in prayer in faith believing
Anytime that you have a need
Call to Him in prayer and you'll be receiving
Even if your faith is as small as a mustard seed
God takes care of His children
We read in the Bible all the time
How God took care of His children
And delivered them from evil every time
God took care of His children
As they wandered thru the Wilderness
Because God takes care of His children
And He always does for them what is best
Oh! God takes care of His children
Takes care of His children everyday
God takes care of His children
My God takes care of His children
And for them He always makes a way
Oh! I'm glad I'm one of His children
I'm one of His children born anew
Oh! I'm glad I'm one of His children

CONNIE J STOUT

I'm on of God's children, how about you?

61

In That Bright City

Mommy, precious mommy and daddy, I
Hate to leave this way
But in that bright city where the streets
Are made of gold
I will wait and watch for you each day
Mommy, precious mommy and daddy, how I
Hate to see you cry
But in that bright city where the gates are
Opened wide
We will never more say good bye
Mommy, precious mommy and daddy, Oh! How I
Love you so
But in that bright city there is one that i
Love more
And when He called for me I had to go
Mommy, precious mommy and daddy, oh, please
Do not cry
For in that bright city where all the children live
You can come and join me by and by
Precious mommy and daddy Jesus called for me

I'll Follow Jesus

I'll follow Jesus, I'll follow Him
I'll follow Jesus, though the path be dim
I'll follow Jesus, I will not stray
I'll follow Jesus, for He'll lead me all the way
I'll follow Jesus, I'll climb that hill
I'll follow Jesus, for He leads me still
I'll follow Jesus, for He'll make a way
I'll follow Jesus, each night and day
I'll follow Jesus, He speaks to me
I'll follow Jesus, even when the trial be
I'll follow Jesus, when I don't understand
I'll follow Jesus, for He holds my hand
Thank You Jesus

March On Pilgrim

March on pilgrim, march on through the night
March on weary pilgrim girded for the fight
Keep on marching pilgrim, God will
Lead the way
Keep on marching pilgrim, through the rough
And rocky road
Just keep on marching, God will share the load
Keep on marching pilgrim, He'll lead you through
The strife
Keep marching weary pilgrim, you'll win
A crown of life
Satan is no match if on this road you trod
Satan has no power at all, when you call upon your God
So keep marching pilgrim, He'll lead you
Through the night
Keep marching weary pilgrim, to God's eternal light
Keep marching pilgrim, God is with you

He Will Hold Me In His Hand

He will hold me in the palm of His hand
He will guide me safely through this land
He will never let me go
Because He loves me so
And He'll keep me in the palm of
His hand

65

Speak Not In Anger

Speak not in anger words that
Cause pain
Those same words may come back to
Haunt you again
No one is perfect, save God above
Speak not in anger to those that you love

God Says To Forgive

God says we must forgive
If for Him we choose to live
We cannot hate our fellow man
And teach them of His loving, saving plan
If we ask forgiveness when we pray
And show no mercy to others on the way
No mercy then shall we receive
No forgiveness from God will be seen
God says to forgive our brothers
If we hope to reach Heaven's shore
If we don't forgive, we won't be forgiven
We must love and forgive if for God
We are living

67

Through The Power Of The Blood

Through the power of the blood I shall overcome
Through the power of the blood I shall overcome
Through the power of the blood I shall overcome
Everything that Satan throws my way
Through the power of the blood I'm victorious
Through the power of the blood I'm victorious
Through the power of the blood I'm victorious
Through the power of the blood I'll overcome
By His blood I am saved
By his stripes I am healed
Although I'm not worthy
He loves me still
He loved me so much, He dies on Calvary
Jesus the Savior shed His blood for all man kind
Yet when He was dying He still remembered me
Through the power of the blood we're saved

68

Drawing Nigh

Be ready oh my soul for the Lord
To call you home
Be ready for that day is drawing nigh
Be ready oh my soul for the Lord to
Call you home
To live with Him forever in the sky
Drawing nigh, drawing nigh
The day of His return is drawing nigh
Drawing nigh, drawing nigh
From the sign of the time it
Drawing nigh

I'm Glad I Have A Savior

I'm so glad I have a Savior who watches
Over me
He leads me and guides me over life's troubled sea
I'm so glad for this Savior, who dies on Calvary
By His stripes I can be healed
By His blood I am cleansed
By His mercy I am saved
From the sin I was living in
By His Power I'll Make It Through

70

Colorado

Colorado, I hear you calling me
Colorado, say come and be free
Say come and ski down my mountain side
Colorado calls me day and night
Colorado with your mountains high
Reaching up into the clear blue sky
Colorado birds sing all the day
Colorado calls from far away

Look At The Fishes

Look at all the little fishes play
Swimming in the water all the day
Swimming and playing and eating all their food
Splashing and playing like fishes do

72

Here Kitty

Here kitty, here kitty come into the house
Hurry dear kitty, I see a mouse
You can catch it dear kitty if you
Hurry I think
Then I'll give you a dish of warm milk
To drink

73

Love Is

Love is patient, love is kind
Love is "ours" nor yours or mine
Love is helping and being there
No matter what, no matter where
So, give love a chance and let it grow
Through good times and bad times love helps
You through it, this I know
Love never sees age or the years that
Come and go
Love only sees the heart, that's all it
Needs to know

74

Jesus Takes Care Of Me

Jesus takes care of me everyday
Jesus takes care of me along the way
He guides my feet and holds my hand
Through this dark, rough and rocky road
Yes, every day in every way, Jesus
Takes care of me

Jesus Signed My Pardon

Get thee behind me Satan
I know what you're trying to do
You're trying to get me to follow you
And that's something I'll never do
Jesus signed my pardon
One day at Calvary
The day that He suffered
And died there on the tree
So, get behind me Satan
I'll never follow you
I'm going home to be with Jesus
No matter what you do
I'll reach that home in Heaven
I know's awaiting me
I'll never follow thee

I'm A Winner

I don't need to buy a ticket for the lotto
I don't need to win a big game show
I don't need a lot of earthly riches for I know
I have Jesus Christ the Lord, now I'm a winner
I'm a winner, I'm a winner
I'm a child of the King
That's worth more than anything
I'm no longer a loser I'm a winner
I don't need a lot of fame, lands and money
That I thought I couldn't do without
I have Jesus Christ the King
He's worth more than anything
I'm no longer a loser, I'm a winner

Send Down You Love Lord

Send down you love Lord
Send it today
Send down you love Lord
Send it we pray
We need your love Lord
To help us get through
Send down you love Lord
We're depending on you
Send down your love Lord
We feel so alone
We need you love Lord
To help lead us home
So send down your love Lord
What more can we say?
Then send down you love Lord
We need it today

When We Meet God's Son

If upon life's weary road
If I can help to ease a load
Then I will feel my work is done
When face to face I meet God's son
So many people here on earth
Don't know what a smile is worth
They never smile at anyone
Will God smile at them when there
Work is done?
So if for someone you walk a mile
When you leave, leave a smile
Then you can feel you work is done
When face to face you meet God's son
Jesus said to "Love one another as I have loved you"

The Lord Is Watching Over Me

I know the Lord is watching, He's
Watching over me
He leads me and keeps me safe, upon
Life's stormy sea
He'll never forsake me if His word I will obey
He's watching me and guiding my footsteps
Day by day
Many time I may stumble as I walk this
Narrow road
Sometimes I almost fall beneath life's
Heavy load
But just when things seem darkest and all
Hope is gone
He gently reminds me that I'll never walk alone
I know the Lord is watching, He's watching over me
I know he keeps me safe upon life's troubled sea
I know he won't forsake me, if for him I live
So, as long as life endures my all to him
I give
Thank You Lord

80

I'm Going Home Someday

I'm going home to Heaven someday
This life is just a stop along the way
Though I walk through many valleys
I know Jesus and a mansion are waiting
In my Heavenly home
Although I sometimes suffer
As I travel on my way
I know my Jesus hears me
And answers when I pray
He walks along beside me
And keeps me safe from harm
And in any time of trouble
He keeps me in the shelter of His arms

In The Still Of The Night

In the still of the night when all is quiet
The Lord speaks to me and restores my soul
In the still of the night when all is quiet
The Lord speaks to me, saying I have need of thee
Tell of the people wherever you go
That I'm coming back and I want them to know
That it won't be very long
Till I come for those that to me belong
In the still of the night when all is quiet
The Lord speaks to me and reassures my soul,
That I've been made whole
Thank You Jesus, Praise Your Hold Name

Let Me Be Ever Ready

I love you Lord Jesus with all of my heart
I love you Lord Jesus please never depart
Out of my heart or out of my life
I love you Lord Jesus in peace and strife
Let me be ever ready though I may stumble
And fall
I want to be ever ready to answer you call
So strengthen my spirit and steady my feet
Keep me ever ready my Savior to meet
Let me help those who would fall by the way
By some act of kindness and the right words to say
Let me be ever ready to seek out the lost
And bring them to Jesus whatever the cost
Let me be ever ready through the night or the day
Let me be ever watchful and ready to pray,
For the lost one's wandering in darkness and sin
So that some lost soul for Christ could win
I Love You Jesus

83

I Love You Lord

I love you Lord more than silver and gold
I love you Lord more than riches untold
I love you Lord and I'll always be,
Willing to be used by thee

Heaven The Beautiful Land

I love you Lord Jesus more than silver or gold
I love you Lord Jesus please help me to be bold
And not to be afraid to speak of your love
And tell everyone there's a Heaven above
That it's waiting up there for me and you
If we live for Jesus we'll make it through
To that beautiful land where there never comes night
To that beautiful land where the Lamb is the light
Where all is peaceful and full of love
In that beautiful land of Heaven above
It can't be purchased by you or me
For the price was paid on Calvary
When Jesus hung on the cross and cried
"Father forgive them" just before He died
Thank You Jesus
I Love You Jesus

I've Been Forgiven

I've been forgiven, I've been forgiven
Yes, my name's in that book
On the judgement day, it won't take
Long to look
To find my name written there in the
Lamb's book of live
When I've made it through all of life's
Trouble and strife
I've been forgiven, I've been forgiven
Yes, my name's in that book
I've been forgiven and it won't take
Long to look
To find my name written there with the
Prophets of old
When I get to that city with streets of
Pure gold

86

I'll Never Give Up

I'll never give up, I'll never stop
I'm going to make it to the top
The top of Mt. Zion, where I can see
Jesus my Savior who died for me
I'll never give up, I'll never stop
I'm going to make it to the top
The top of Mt. Zion, that city square
And meet my loved one awaiting me there
Though Satan tries to make me stop
I'm going to make it to the top
The top of Mt. Zion where I will be
Through endless ages shouting victory

87

Hold To My Hand

Hold to my hand, hold to my hand
Don't let me fall back into life's sinking sand
Where I'd be lost forever more
Hold to my hand till I reach Heavens shore
Sometimes I stumble, sometimes I fall
And when I do, on your name I call
You give me the strength to get up
And try again
Through all of life's sorrows, Lord
Hold to my hand
Thank you Lord for holding my
Hand and bringing me through
So much
I Love You Lord!

I Speak Peace To You

When you're sad and you're lonely, and you're
Burdened down to
In the name of the Father I speak peace to you
I speak peace to you child, I speak peace to you
In the name of the Father I speak peace to you
In the name of the Father and His
Son Jesus I speak peace to you.

89

God's Comforting Ways

A shelter in the storm
A resting place in the night
A helping hand when you're down
These are God's comforting ways
A gentle hand to dry our tears
Peace and strength when our heart fears
Hope when all is gone
These are God's comforting ways
To walk beside us through the trials
Trust God He is our redeemer and savior

90

I'll Make It Through

I'll not give up the fight till Glory Land I see
I'll not give up the fight because Jesus
Walks with me
I'll make it through no matter what comes my way
I'll make it through to Glory Land someday
By the love and grace of God
I'll make it through

Praise Him

His praise shall continually be in my mouth,
Whether I travel east, west, north or south
For he alone is worthy to be praised
I'll serve and praise him for the
Rest of my days
I love You Jesus
Thank You

I'll Take Jesus

There is on one like my Jesus in this world
No one like my Jesus in this world
There is no one like my Jesus, my Savior and my Lord
There is no one like my Jesus in this world
No one can take the place of Jesus in my heart
No one can take the place of Jesus in my heart
No one can take the place of Jesus, for the
Joy He does impart
No one can take the place of Jesus in my heart
I tell you now old Satan you have lost
I tell you now old Satan you have lost
I'll serve my Jesus, for He paid the cost
I tell you now old Satan you have lost!
Jesus is my Lord and Savior
Thank You Jesus
I Love You Jesus

Praise The Name Of Jesus

Praise the name of Jesus, worship and
Adore him
Praise the name of Jesus, worship and
Adore him
Put no one else before Him
Praise the precious name of Jesus, the one
Who made me whole
Praise the name of Jesus, the one
Who made me whole
He is the keeper of my soul
Praise the precious name of Jesus,
He is my all in all
Praise the name of Jesus, He is my all in all
He hears me each time I call
And He answers my prayers
Thank you Jesus for being there
Thank you Jesus, I know you care

94

Darkness Has To Go

The dark clouds hung over me every
Night and day
Clouds that were so dark I could not
See the way
Then one day Jesus said, the darkness
Has to go
And now I walk in sunshine
Everywhere I go
Now I walk in sunshine the darkness
Is no more
Now I walk in sunshine
Thank you Lord

God's Only Son

In a tomb He was laid out
But death could not hold him
He was God's only son
In the world below
On a cross He fulfilled the plan
Of Salvation
I want to thank my Jesus
For He's coming again

96

The Choice

God made a choice when He decided to send
His only son down here below
Yes the choice to send His only son
Down here below
He chose to send His one and only son
To die for a world so lost in sin
It hurt so much to see them beating Him
His paid and sorrow must have hurt the Father so
BUT
He chose to save a lost and dying world
From torment through eternity for living so sinfully
I'm glad that He let Him take the place for me
I'm thankful for the choice He made
Jesus chose to obey His Father's will
He said "not my will but thine be done"
I decided one night to follow Jesus
And to give Him my heart and my all
God never fails me when I call Him
He always hears and answers my prayers
He takes away all my heartaches and cares
The choice was the best I ever made
YES
I made a choice and decided to live
For God while here below

97

Jesus Can

Jesus can heal you no matter what you have
Have faith, believe and ask in His name
Jesus can save you no matter what you have done
And your life will never be the same
Yes, there'll be trials and temptations and burdens
You must bear
If you have faith, He will help you through it all
He will walk beside you and hold your hand
And He will never let you fall
When earthly friends forsake you and refuse to
Shake your hand
Jesus will always be right there
Jesus will love you no matter what you've done
He is a friend who'll always care
Jesus will forgive all your sins,
And never will forsake you

Jesus Has Promised A Mansion To Me

Jesus has promised a mansion to me
Where I will live throughout eternity
No paid, no suffering, no tears will be shed
For Jesus paid the debt when His precious
Blood was shed
My Jesus loves me just as I am
As long as I obey His command
He doesn't care how I look
As long as I obey the rules in His book

99

The Lord Made The World

The Lord made the world to hand in space
Then He put the stars in place
On this earth there is not one
Who can do what the Lord has done
The Lord created the Heaven and earth
And through His trouble it would be worth
But later on He was very sad
Because the people in this world were bad
In His own image God made man
And placed him caretaker over His
Beautiful land
The Lord made woman and called her Eve
But, by old Satan she was deceived
They could eat of all they did see
They could eat of all except one tree
But they did eat and disobey
And by the Lord they were sent away
The Lord made it rain 40 days and nights
The water rose to mighty heights
Through the waters a large vessel came
With man and his family,
Noah was his name

100

All Is Well

When things are bad and I cannot cope
Jesus speaks peace and gives to me hope
All is well, all is well, He says to me
When my soul is cast down
And I cannot find my way
Jesus says don't cry, don't feel down
All is well, all is well, when you pray
All is well, all is well
Jesus came to tell us, all is well
All is well, all is well
With Jesus as our savior all is well

101

When He calls Me Home

My Jesus died so I might live
All my heart to Him I give
Never more in Sin I'll roam
I'll serve Him till He calls me home
When He calls me home, when He calls me home
How I'll rejoice when He calls me home
When He calls me home, when He calls me home
What joys we'll share when He calls me home
I can hardly wait till He calls me home
When I feel my burdens get me down
I think of Jesus and the thorn made crown
He wore for me upon His head
And His precious blood for me He shed
He let them nail Him to the cross
So my soul would not be lost
Is it any wonder that I say

103

Faith Hope and Love

Faith Hope and Love in Jesus Above
When all else seems gone, these three remain
Faith hope and Love in Jesus above
Faith through life's storms in Jesus above
When life Is a tempest, have faith in His name
Through faith in His name you will stand through the day
Hope for tomorrow form Jesus Above
His Hope for tomorrow, blots out this day's sorrow
Hope for tomorrow from Jesus above
Love never failing form Jesus above
Love Never ending from Jesus above
His Love will never forsake me form Jesus above.
Faith Hope and Love form Jesus above
Faith Hope and Love, and the greatest His Love.

Milton Keynes UK
Ingram Content Group UK Ltd.
UKHW022322030424
440511UK00005B/233